EYEWITNESS TO HISTORY

MAJOR CULTURAL MOVEMENTS

Inside the WITHDRAWN

LGBTQ+ MOVEMENT

LESBIAN NOW RIGHTS

By Jennifer Lombardo

Gareth Stevens
PUBLISHING

Please visit our website, www.garethstevens.com. For a free color catalog of all our high-quality books, call toll free 1-800-542-2595 or fax 1-877-542-2596.

Cataloging-in-Publication Data

Names: Lombardo, Jennifer.
Title: Inside the LGBTQ+ movement / Jennifer Lombardo.
Description: New York : Gareth Stevens Publishing, 2018. | Series: Eyewitness to history: major cultural movements | Includes index.
Identifiers: LCCN ISBN 9781538211656 (pbk.) | ISBN 9781538211670 (library bound) | ISBN 9781538211663 (6 pack)
Subjects: LCSH: Sexual minorities–Juvenile literature. | Sexual minorities–Civil rights–United States–Juvenile literature. | Sexual minority youth–Juvenile literature.
Classification: LCC HQ73.L63 2018 | DDC 306.76–dc23

First Edition

Published in 2018 by
Gareth Stevens Publishing
111 East 14th Street, Suite 349
New York, NY 10003

Copyright © 2018 Gareth Stevens Publishing

Designer: Katelyn E. Reynolds
Editor: Therese Shea

Photo credits: Cover, p. 1 (person) Robert Sherbow/The LIFE Images Collection/Getty Images; cover, p. 1 (background image) Porter Gifford/Liaison/Getty Images; cover, p. 1 (logo quill icon) Seamartini Graphics Media/Shutterstock.com; cover, p. 1 (logo stamp) YasnaTen/Shutterstock.com; cover, p. 1 (color grunge frame) DmitryPrudnichenko/Shutterstock.com; cover, pp. 1–32 (paper background) Nella/Shutterstock.com; cover, pp. 1–32 (decorative elements) Ozerina Anna/Shutterstock.com; pp. 1–32 (wood texture) Reinhold Leitner/Shutterstock.com; pp. 1–32 (open book background) Elena Schweitzer/Shutterstock.com; pp. 1–32 (bookmark) Robert Adrian Hillman/Shutterstock.com; p. 5 © iStockphoto.com/MarijaRadovic ; p. 7 Ajkeating/Wikipedia.org; p. 9 Prosfilaes/Wikipedia.org; p. 11 (top) Louis Liotta / (c) NYP Holdings, Inc. via Getty Images; p. 11 (bottom) Diana Davies, copyright owned by New York Public Library/Wikipedia.org; p. 13 Mark Reinstein/Corbis via Getty Images; p. 15 Barbara Alper/Getty Images; p. 17 Bettmann/Getty Images; p. 19 BRENDAN SMIALOWSKI/AFP/Getty Images; p. 21 EMMANUEL DUNAND/AFP/Getty Images; p. 23 David McNew/Getty Images; p. 25 Sara D. Davis/Getty Images; p. 27 SpeedKingz/Shutterstock.com

Printed in the United States of America

CPSIA compliance information: Batch #CW18GS: For further information contact Gareth Stevens, New York, New York at 1-800-542-2595.

CONTENTS

*Words in the glossary appear in **bold** type the first time they are used in the text.*

A LONG *Fight*

Although people who identify as lesbian, gay, bisexual, transgender, or another type of **sexual orientation** or **gender** identity have always existed, they have often had to hide who they were. In the United States, being gay was once illegal; if police thought two people of the same sex were more than just friends, both were arrested. For a long time, many people wrongly believed that being gay was a choice. Some still do.

The LGBTQ+ movement is the fight for the rights and respect that heterosexual people have always enjoyed. Some heroic individuals have led the effort for acceptance, which is still in motion. Harvey Fierstein, an actor and **activist**, encouraged the LGBTQ+ community: *"Never be bullied into silence. . . . Accept no one's definition of your life; define yourself."*

LGBTQ+ people are just like everyone else, but they've struggled with acceptance in society.

WHAT DOES LGBTQ+ MEAN?

"LGBTQ" is a term for the community that includes those who identify as lesbian, gay, bisexual (attracted to both men and women), transgender (identity different from gender labeled at birth), and queer (not heterosexual or not **conforming** to a gender role) or questioning (unsure of label). But there are others in this community, such as those who describe themselves as intersex (physically not clearly male or female) and asexual (no sexual orientation). To be **inclusive**, we use the term "LGBTQ+" in this book.

"Heteronormativity" is the view that being heterosexual is the normal or preferred sexual orientation. It can make people who are LGBTQ+ feel like they're viewed as unnatural. It has influenced everything in society, including gender norms, which are ideas about gender that many people believe. For example, a boy's parents may not let him play with dolls because they think only girls should play with dolls. People are now realizing gender norms aren't supported by science and heteronormativity is harmful to a large community of individuals.

Attitudes have been slow to change. It's only recently that many people have begun to accept those in the LGBTQ+ community. This is thanks to years of activists fighting against **discrimination** and outdated ideas.

MORE TO KNOW

Famous people have been victims of discrimination based on their sexual orientation. Oscar Wilde, author of *The Picture of Dorian Gray* and *The Importance of Being Earnest*, was jailed in England from 1895 to 1897 for homosexual behavior.

Founded in 1996, Out & Equal has headquarters in San Francisco, California. It provides training and resources for both LGBTQ+ employees and the businesses they work for.

THE FIRST
Gay Rights Organization

Years ago, it took a lot of courage for anyone in the LGBTQ+ community to speak up for themselves when they knew they could be punished for it. The first gay rights organization—the Society for Human Rights—was created in 1924 by Henry Gerber. Gerber decided to start the group after the US Army sent him to Germany in 1919, following World War I. He saw how much better things were for LGBTQ+ people there. They had more freedom to be themselves.

Gerber said, *"I had always bitterly felt the injustice with which my own American society accused the homosexual of 'immoral acts.'"* Sadly, not many people joined the Society for Human Rights, and the organization had disbanded by 1925.

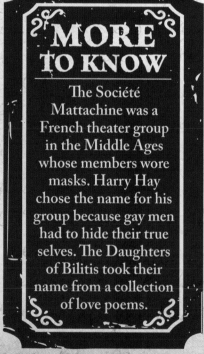

MORE TO KNOW

The Société Mattachine was a French theater group in the Middle Ages whose members wore masks. Harry Hay chose the name for his group because gay men had to hide their true selves. The Daughters of Bilitis took their name from a collection of love poems.

The Ladder was published by the Daughters of Bilitis from 1956 to 1972.

The Ladder
OCTOBER, 1957

In the 1920s, there was still too much antigay opinion for the Society for Human Rights to be successful. By the 1950s, although the LGBTQ+ community was still not widely accepted in society, attitudes had changed enough for two new organizations to have better luck attracting members. The Mattachine Society was founded for gay men in 1950 by activist Harry Hay, and the Daughters of Bilitis was established for lesbians in 1955 by Phyllis Lyon and Del Martin.

The STONEWALL *Riots*

The 1950s and 1960s were a time when some groups that had been discriminated against for a long time fought back in large numbers. The civil rights movement battled for equality for black people during this period. Even though their fight continues today, African Americans made great improvements by 1968, including federal laws against discrimination. The LGBTQ+ community began to demand equal rights partly because of the success of the black civil rights movement.

On June 28, 1969, police raided a gay bar in New York City called the Stonewall Inn. The police behaved violently toward many of the Stonewall patrons, and several people were arrested. The Stonewall Inn was the third gay bar in the area to be **raided** in a short period of time, and the LGBTQ+ community had become resentful and angry. Instead of running away from the police, a crowd began to fight back, yelling and throwing objects.

Dick Leitsch, a member of the Mattachine Society and a gay journalist, explained, *"The Stonewall became 'home' to these kids. When it was raided, they fought for it."* For the next 5 days, mobs **rioted** in Greenwich Village. These riots were the starting point of the modern LGBTQ+ rights movement.

MORE TO KNOW

At a time when the drinking age was 18, certain bars allowed LGBTQ+ teenagers to meet other people like themselves in a place where their true identities were accepted.

The Stonewall Inn was an important gathering place for many LGBTQ+ people in the late 1960s.

PARADES
and Marches

On June 28, 1970, members of the LGBTQ+ community marched through the streets of New York City in memory of the Stonewall riots the year before. The event became known as Christopher Street Liberation Day and is considered the first gay pride parade. Similar parades have been held every year across the country since then.

On October 14, 1979, the first National March on Washington for Lesbian and Gay Rights took place. More than 75,000 marchers demanded civil rights laws for LGBTQ+ people. Activist Frank Kameny explained one reason for marching: *"I will define myself to my government. I will not allow my government to define me to me. . . . We citizens are the masters; the government are our servants, not the other way round."*

FRANK KAMENY

Frank Kameny (1925–2011) graduated from Harvard University and worked as an astronomer for the Army Map Service until he was fired in 1957 for being gay. He fought back in court. Though unsuccessful, it was the first US court case of its kind. It made him determined to help make life better for others in the LGBTQ+ community. Kameny's actions were inspired by Martin Luther King Jr.'s nonviolent protests.

The march on Washington helped to unify the LGBTQ+ movement across the country. Previously, the struggle for rights had been local.

MORE TO KNOW

In 1961, Illinois became the first state to **repeal** its antigay laws.

EARLY
Achievements

Even though LGBTQ+ people are still fighting for rights today, they did have some successes soon after their movement started. In 1973, the American Psychiatric Association stated there was no scientific evidence that homosexuality was a mental illness, as had been previously claimed. At the time, the "cures" for homosexuality included electric shock therapy.

In 1974, Kathy Kozachenko and Elaine Noble became the first two openly gay people to be elected to political office. Kozachenko said, *"Many people's attitudes about gayness are still far from healthy, but my campaign forced some people at least to re-examine their prejudices and stereotypes [labels]."*

In 1975, the first federal gay rights bill was

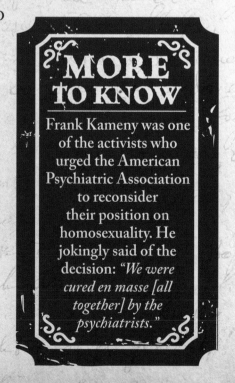

MORE TO KNOW

Frank Kameny was one of the activists who urged the American Psychiatric Association to reconsider their position on homosexuality. He jokingly said of the decision: *"We were cured en masse [all together] by the psychiatrists."*

introduced to Congress. The bill would have protected LGBTQ+ people from discrimination, but didn't gain enough support in Congress to become law.

The AIDS outbreak was marked by inaccurate reports about how the disease was spread. Thankfully, research led to breakthroughs in education and treatment.

THE AIDS CRISIS

In the 1980s, many gay men contracted AIDS (acquired immune deficiency syndrome), a disease that makes it harder for the body to fight off illness. Even though anyone can get AIDS, gay men are at a higher risk. Some who were against the LGBTQ+ community said gay men were being punished for the way they lived. Until people protested, scientists weren't given enough money to research cures. Drugs have been created to help people with the disease live much longer now.

FACING *Violence*

HARVEY MILK

As a young man, Harvey Milk worked as a public school teacher, investment banker, and Broadway musical production coordinator in New York City. In 1972, he moved to San Francisco, California, and opened a camera shop. In 1973, he first ran for office, but lost. He was finally elected in 1977 to the San Francisco City-County Board. His **assassination** was a blow to the LGBTQ+ community, who remembered all the good he had wanted to do.

LGBTQ+ people have always been at higher risk for violence than others. They're more likely to be bullied at school, and sometimes they've even been killed just because of their sexual orientation or gender identity. This fact became difficult for Americans to ignore in 1978, when gay politician Harvey Milk was murdered.

In 1977, Milk was the first openly gay person elected to public office in California. He believed, *"All young people, regardless of sexual orientation or identity, deserve a safe and supportive environment in which to achieve their full potential [promise]."* He worked toward that kind of community in San Francisco. However, a man named Dan White shot Milk 1 year after he was elected because White believed LGBTQ+ people were a threat to society.

Dan White, Harvey Milk's killer, had been a member of the San Francisco Board of Supervisors. Many were angry that White was sentenced to only 7 years in prison for his crime.

MORE TO KNOW

In 1995, the Hate Crimes Sentencing Enhancement Act made penalties for crimes worse if it was proven that someone was hurt or killed based on characteristics including sexual orientation or gender identity.

Harvey Milk

Violence against the LGBTQ+ community continued through the decades in the United States. On June 12, 2016, the deadliest mass shooting in US history occurred at Pulse, a gay nightclub in Orlando, Florida. A man named Omar Mateen killed 49 people and injured more than 50 before police killed him. Based on Mateen's personal history, the police believe he acted out of hatred for the LGBTQ+ community.

Michelangelo Signorile of the *HuffPost* reminded the nation that violence against LGBTQ+ people wasn't new: *"The brutal reality that jarred Orlando's LGBT community, and the entire nation, is something that LGBT people have always experienced . . . it's a reminder of the animus [hatred] against LGBT people that still exists, and the ever present danger with which we still live."*

MORE TO KNOW

In 2009, a federal law called the Matthew Shepard Act was signed. It made attacking an individual because of sexual orientation or gender identity a federal crime. It was named for Matthew Shepard, a gay man beaten to death in Laramie, Wyoming, in 1998.

After the shooting at Pulse nightclub, people of all sexual orientations showed their support for the LGBTQ+ community. Gatherings of support were held across the country.

BEING AN ALLY

An ally is someone who stands up for people even when an issue doesn't affect them personally. People who aren't LGBTQ+ can be allies by listening to LGBTQ+ people, going to marches and protests, and doing their best to show love and support for those in the community. Some schools even have groups for allies and people who are LGBTQ+ to meet and work together.

THE RIGHT
to Marry

In 1996, the LGBTQ+ movement saw a major setback. President Bill Clinton signed the Defense of Marriage Act (DOMA), which defined marriage for federal purposes as the union of one man and one woman. The federal government wouldn't recognize marriage between those of the same sex.

Even though the federal law had passed, individual states weren't prevented from deciding whether or not same-sex couples could legally marry. In fact, a Hawaiian judge ruled in 1996 that gay and lesbian couples should be allowed to marry in Hawaii. While this was a victory, legally married couples who moved to another state could lose their married status, since DOMA also allowed states to refuse to accept same-sex marriages granted under the laws of other states.

DON'T ASK, DON'T TELL

During World War II, the United States banned homosexuals from serving in the armed forces. In 1993, President Bill Clinton signed the Don't Ask, Don't Tell (DADT) law, which said gays, lesbians, and bisexuals could serve in the military if no one knew their sexual orientation. This was stressful for LGBTQ+ service members, who could have been discharged if they were discovered. President Barack Obama signed DADT's repeal in 2011. In 2017, however, President Donald Trump tried to stop those who are transgender from serving in the military.

MORE TO KNOW

Lawyers for the state of Hawaii argued children were best raised by two heterosexual parents. However, experts agreed that gay couples could raise children just as well, especially if they could wed.

Many same-sex couples demanded the repeal of the Defense of Marriage Act.

MARRIAGE IS A HUMAN RIGHT NOT A HETEROSEXUAL PRIVILEGE!

"I DO" SUPPORT THE FREEDOM TO MARRY

One by one, states began to allow gay and lesbian couples to marry. Some only allowed them to have a civil union, which is similar to a marriage, but doesn't give couples as many rights and benefits, such as tax breaks. Many people didn't agree with gay marriage because they thought it was wrong, but slowly attitudes changed.

After Maryland state delegate Wade Kach met some same-sex couples, he said, *"I saw with so many of the gay couples, they were so devoted to [one] another. I saw so much love. When this hearing was over, I was a changed person in regard to this issue."* Finally, in June 2015, the Supreme Court ruled that the US government and states weren't allowed to ban gay marriage.

MORE TO KNOW

The hashtag #LoveWins became popular when gay marriage was legalized in all 50 states.

In June 2015, same-sex marriage was made legal across the country. The LGBTQ+ community celebrated a major victory.

WHY IS MARRIAGE IMPORTANT?

Some people don't think marriage matters much, but it's important for many reasons. It gives couples certain rights that unmarried people don't have. For example, if a person needs to be in a hospital, often only a spouse, or husband or wife, can stay with them during restricted visiting hours. Married people can receive insurance benefits through their spouse's employer. They can also take time off to care for their spouse when they're ill.

23

BATHROOM *Bills*

LOOKING FOR JUSTICE

When people break laws that protect the rights of LGBTQ+ people, the matter may be taken to court. In 2012, Colorado bakery owner Jack Phillips refused to bake a wedding cake for David Mullins and Charlie Craig because Phillips said his religion disapproved of LGBTQ+ couples. The Colorado Civil Rights Commission ruled this was discrimination. Louise Melling of the American Civil Liberties Union said, *"Religious liberty gives you the right to your beliefs but not the right to harm others."*

In the 2010s, several states proposed bills that would force people to use the bathroom or locker room that matches the sex on their birth certificate rather than the gender they identify with. People who agree with these laws often say they're needed to protect children from transgender people or people who are pretending to be transgender. In reality, bathroom laws harm transgender people by falsely making them seem scary. They may also subject them to **harassment** and even danger in the bathrooms corresponding to their biological sex.

Transgender actress Laverne Cox said, *"Those who oppose trans people having access to the facilities consistent with how we identify know that all the things they claim don't actually happen. It's really about us not existing—about erasing trans people."*

Some businesses that don't support proposed "bathroom laws" have made bathrooms gender neutral so everyone can use them.

We do not discriminate.
We oppose HB2.

#WeAreNotThis

IN THE AGE
of the Internet

In some ways, the internet has made life easier for LGBTQ+ people. Chat rooms and websites have made it simpler and safer for LGBTQ+ people to connect with each other and offer support. They can find information about issues they may not feel comfortable asking their parents or teachers about. But LGBTQ+ people are also more likely to be bullied, and the internet has made it easier for bullies to target them.

Cyberbullying is hard to escape. LGBTQ+ teens have even killed themselves because of it. Ellen DeGeneres is one of many celebrities and activists who have spoken out about this. She said, *"I want anyone out there who feels different and alone to know that I know how you feel, and there is help out there."*

MORE TO KNOW

Every year, the Gay, Lesbian and Straight Education Network (GLSEN) organizes a Day of Silence to make people aware of the harassment LGBTQ+ students face. Anyone can take part.

Cyberbullying, just like face-to-face bullying, can have damaging effects on LGBTQ+ people. In many states, cyberbullying is against the law. This includes threatening messages sent through email, text, social media, and other forms of online communication.

7 CUPS

A website called 7 Cups of Tea (www.7cups.com) is an online emotional support service. It allows people to chat **anonymously** with trained listeners—people who have taken a course on how to encourage someone to talk about their problems. The website also has forums in which users can chat with and support each other, including some specifically for the LGBTQ+ community, so they can communicate with others who understand what they're going through.

FUTURE *Challenges*

The LGBTQ+ community has come a long way in a few decades, but there's more work to be done. More laws need to be passed to protect civil rights, and society's attitude toward LGBTQ+ people needs to change more. But no law can change an attitude; this is why the LGBTQ+ community needs allies to join the fight.

Noah Michaelson, the founding editor of *HuffPost* Gay Voices, said: *"We can pass all the laws we want and talk about public policy until we run out of air, but until our society stops thinking of [LGBTQ+] people as deviant [abnormal] or corrupt or sinful or in any way less than [non–LGBTQ+] people, nothing is going to change . . . We need to talk openly and honestly about our lives and who we love."*

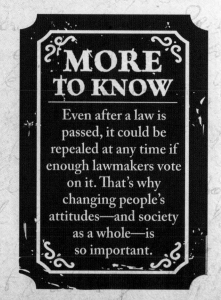

MORE TO KNOW

Even after a law is passed, it could be repealed at any time if enough lawmakers vote on it. That's why changing people's attitudes—and society as a whole—is so important.

TIMELINE
THE STRUGGLE FOR LGBTQ+ RIGHTS

1924 — The first gay rights group, the Society for Human Rights, is created.

1961 — Illinois becomes the first state to repeal its anti-gay laws.

1969 — Police raid the Stonewall Inn, touching off riots and the birth of the modern gay rights movement.

1970 — The first pride parade is held in New York City.

1973 — The American Psychiatric Association states there's no scientific evidence that homosexuality is a mental disorder.

1974 — Kathy Kozachenko becomes the first openly gay person elected to public office.

1978 — Harvey Milk, the first openly gay person elected to public office in California, is killed.

1979 — The first National March on Washington for Lesbian and Gay Rights takes place.

1993 — President Bill Clinton signs the Don't Ask, Don't Tell law.

1995 — The Hate Crimes Sentencing Enhancement Act makes punishments harsher for criminals who target LGBTQ+ people.

2009 — The Matthew Shepard Act makes attacking an individual because of sexual orientation or gender identity a federal crime.

2010 — President Barack Obama signs the repeal of the Don't Ask, Don't Tell law.

2015 — Gay marriage is legalized across the United States.

2016 — The deadliest mass shooting in US history occurs at Pulse, a gay nightclub, in Orlando, Florida.

LAMBDA LEGAL

Lambda Legal is a nonprofit organization that was founded in 1973 to help LGBTQ+ people fight for their rights. It does this by giving free legal help and by educating the LGBTQ+ community about the rights they already have. Lambda Legal wants to make sure LGBTQ+ people know their rights so others cannot take advantage of them. The organization also works with local and national lawmakers to change laws that harm the LGBTQ+ community.

GLOSSARY

activist: a person who uses or supports strong actions to help make changes in politics or society

anonymously: in a manner in which someone isn't identified or made known

assassination: the killing of a public figure

conform: to agree with

discrimination: unfairly treating people unequally because of their race, beliefs, or ways of life

gender: the state of being male or female

harassment: the act of annoying or bothering in a constant or repeated way

inclusive: not limited to certain people

raid: an occurrence in which police suddenly enter a place in a forceful way to find criminals

repeal: to officially make a law no longer valid

riot: creating a public disturbance in which a group of angry people become out of control

sexual orientation: a person's sexual preference

FOR MORE
Information

Books

Penne, Barbra. *Transgender Role Models and Pioneers*. New York, NY: Rosen Publishing, 2017.

Pohlen, Jerome. *Gay & Lesbian History for Kids: The Century-Long Struggle for LGBT Rights, with 21 Activities*. Chicago, IL: Chicago Review Press, 2016.

Watson, Stephanie. *Gay Rights Movement*. Minneapolis, MN: ABDO Publishing Company, 2014.

Websites

GLAAD

glaad.org

This website gives resources for young LGBTQ+ people and their allies.

GLSEN

glsen.org

GLSEN seeks to end discrimination and bullying in schools.

PFLAG

pflag.org

This website provides information to family and friends to help them support their LGBTQ+ loved ones.

INDEX